MW01603229

Intangible Value

Case Studies for How Arts and Sports Can Lead to Business Success

Kevin Wilhelm and Annie Thomas
With Katie Thompson and Ruth Lee

Sustainable
Business Consulting

Printed in the United States of America

First Printing, 2017

ISBN 978-1-365-82668-9

Sustainable Business Consulting
4700 42nd Ave SW, Suite 535
Seattle, WA 98116

http://sustainablebizconsulting.com/

Contents

About the Authors

All four of the authors work for Sustainable Business Consulting (SBC) in Seattle, Washington. The firm strives to help lead, inspire and empower businesses and individuals to change the world, by helping organizations realize business value from their sustainability efforts.

Together, the four of us were reflecting one day about how many of our habits and characteristics were developed during our formative years through the performing arts and by playing sports. So, we thought it would be fun to put a book together to help others recognize how their talents, skills and lessons learned through both sports and the arts are extremely applicable in their professional lives.

This is our second book written as a team, with Annie Thomas and Kevin Wilhelm serving as the lead authors. Our first collective book, *Sustainability Jobs—The Complete Guide to Landing Your Dream, Green Job*, was designed to help young professionals and job seekers find meaningful work.

Kevin Wilhelm is the CEO of Sustainable Business Consulting and is one of the world's pre-eminent business consultants and teachers in the field of sustainability. He has 21+ years of experience working with 115+ businesses ranging across 37 different industries—from Fortune 500 multinationals to small businesses, from government agencies to non-profits. He has also taught sustainability at 12 different Colleges and Universities.

Kevin played three sports in college—soccer, rugby and diving. He is also an all-around sports fanatic. Artistically, he started acting early on and was in his first college play at age 10. He is a Thespian, having been in a concert choir for six years and participated in a singing and dance company in high school, and was even a performing pianist for ten years. He has pretty much hung up his artistic stripes and has retired from competitive sports, but continues to use the lessons he learned from both arts and sports in his daily life.

Kevin is also the author of three acclaimed books, including:
- *Sustainability Jobs: The Complete Guide to Landing Your Dream Green Job* (2016)

- *Making Sustainability Stick: The Blueprint for Successful Sustainability Implementation* (2013)
- *Return on Sustainability: How Business Can Increase Profitability & Address Climate Change in an Uncertain Economy* (2009)

He has also been a contributing writer on five other publications, including:
- *The Reducetarian Solution* (2017)
- *Introduction to Sustainable Business* (2015) Video textbook available on Safari Books only
- *Go Green Rating Scale for Early Childhood Settings* (2010)
- *Green Jobs: A Guide to Eco-Friendly Employment* (2008)
- *Advancing Sustainability in Higher Education* (2007)

Annie Thomas is an Associate at SBC and was the co-author of this book. She is an alumnus of Seattle Pacific University (SPU) with a background in psychology and a M.A. in Sustainable Management. Annie is in her second year at Sustainable Business Consulting and has conducted extensive sustainability research on various client projects as well as helped assess where clients fall on the sustainability spectrum in comparison to others in their industry.

Annie was also a collegiate athlete having played on the Women's Soccer team at SPU. During her college career, Annie served as a captain to her team for her junior and part of her senior year. Artistically, she grew up as a singer and solo artist that gave many performances to large audiences. Additionally, she traveled to Tennessee as a recording artist. Due to multiple knee injuries, Annie has retired from competitive athletics though she still draws from these experiences daily. She also no longer performs artistically but the skills she gained from this time of her life come in handy in her professional life.

This is Annie's second book, having been a co-author on:
- *Sustainability Jobs: The Complete Guide to Landing Your Dream Green Job* (2016)

Ruth Lee is a Senior Consultant and Co-Owner of Sustainable Business Consulting, with 8+ years of experience helping clients develop and implement sustainability strategy, conduct stakeholder engagement to assess materiality, navigate executive level buy-in and manage greenhouse gas emissions. Additionally, she specializes in data analysis, performance indicator measurement, carbon footprinting, and responding to public reporting programs such as the Climate Registry and the Carbon Disclosure Project. She graduated from the University of Washington with a degree in Community, Environment and Planning.

Ruth spent much of her youth as a classically trained pianist but found immense joy and satisfaction when she switched to improvisation and was able to explore her creativity in the space. In addition, Ruth played tennis for her high school and played in tournaments throughout the Pacific Northwest until she retired before attending college.

This is Ruth's second book, having been a co-author on:
- *Sustainability Jobs: The Complete Guide to Landing Your Dream Green Job* (2016)

Katie Thompson is an Associate at Sustainable Business Consulting. She specializes in sustainability strategy and implementation and developing employee engagement techniques. She also has experience helping clients determine their competitive advantage and communicate their sustainability efforts through reporting by conducting carbon emission analyses and industry benchmarking research. She graduated from Western Washington University with a Bachelor of Arts in Business and Sustainability.

Katie grew up as a multi-sport athlete, playing on all types of teams until high school where she settled into volleyball as her main sport. She was co-captain on both her school and club teams for most of those years and even had the opportunity to coach a 14-year-old team during her senior year before retiring from the sport. Katie's high school team won the State Championship her sophomore year and had two more close run-ins with the state title the following two seasons. Her artistic experience with percussion was short-lived, only playing for two years in the middle school band, but music has always been close to her heart.

This is Katie's second book, having been a co-author on:
- *Sustainability Jobs: The Complete Guide to Landing Your Dream Green Job* (2016)

Introduction

We wrote this book because time and time again in our lives, we've realized that much of the groundwork for the keys to our success, both in business and in life, were laid in our youth by performing in the arts and by playing sports.

Kevin had been talking about this in the office, and when he asked us if we had similar experiences, we all began jumping in with our own anecdotes. In both sports and arts, you learn not only the hard skills, but the intangibles that are often hard to quantify, yet are what truly separate the average from the great. The four of us, Kevin Wilhelm, Annie Thomas, Ruth Lee and Katie Thompson pulled together these stories from our own life experiences to be illustrative case studies for how sports and arts helped us develop the tools, mindset, and skills to be successful in the business world. What started out as an idea for a single blog became more, and that is when we came up with the idea of this book: *Intangible Value—Case Studies for How Sports and Arts Can Lead to Business Success.*

We realized that if this was true for us, then it was probably true for many people in the world, and nobody was talking about it. Sure, in the sporting world there are former Olympians and professional athletes who are renowned for their hard work, determination and effort they put in to be the greatest, but what about the rest of us? What about those of us who struggled to learn an instrument but were determined to overcome or those of us who were average athletes that had challenges and tests of character that became fundamental as to whom we became? The majority of us played an instrument or sport at one time in our lives but no longer do so because of a lack of time, desire, ability or just because we now have new interests, hobbies and priorities.

Ask yourself, how did your experiences growing up in music, art, or drama set you up for success? Or if you were an athlete, how did your struggles, wins and losses better prepare you for the real world?

For example, when explaining in a job interview once what kind of team Kevin wanted to be a part of, he used a sports analogy. He used the example of being on a team where everyone always sprinted for the loose ball because he knew he was motivated by people putting in the extra effort and he hoped to do the same—and that there was a culture where this was the expectation, not the exception. That was the type of business team he wanted to work for, and he had no way to explain it other than by using a sports metaphor.

That is the point of this book. Too often people are asked questions during an interview or through their career like, "What are some of the secrets to your success?" but rarely do people talk about their experiences from sports or arts. We wanted to call attention to these anecdotes and remind people, just like we had to learn, that many of the soft skills that you learn early in your life in either arts or sports are things that you can apply to your daily personal and professional life. Good luck. We know that at some point you will see a little bit of yourself in one or more of our stories and we hope it will enable you to remember or apply what you learned earlier in your life to the challenges you face at work today.

Section One: How Art Can Influence Your Business Career

Rarely do you hear a business person say that their success was due to their hard work in the performing arts. Sure, you might hear them attribute it to sports, politics, the military, their parental upbringing, but rarely the performing arts. Why is that? Is it because they tend to put less value on the arts, or don't see the direct connection? Is it because it doesn't sound macho enough to attribute success to playing the piano or being in the concert choir? Yet, why do so many business women and men end up supporting the arts financially once they've achieved success?

Our belief is that whether you were involved in the arts at a young age, in high school or college, that the skills learned through the performing arts are directly applicable to daily business situations. In fact, we believe that the arts can be one of the most helpful teaching instruments (no pun intended) for anyone hoping to excel in the corporate world.

The goal of this section of the book is to begin to change the mindset of people in the corporate world as it relates to arts. Hopefully the learnings and stories presented here can help demonstrate to young professionals, hiring managers, recruiters, parents and even students that the skills learned in the performing arts directly translate into business.

The four of us have filled this book with stories, tips, lessons learned and illustrative examples from our combined years of experience practicing and performing in the arts: in music, drama and improv whether it be as soloists, part of an ensemble, on a stage or part of a band. If you've ever participated in the performing arts, we hope that these short stories will enable you to recognize that the values, work ethic and habits you formed can be a positive influence in being successful in your day to day life—at work, at home, and as a parent or friend. If you are a hiring manager, boss or recruiter, but you've never participated in the arts, we want you to have a better understanding as to how exactly the attributes of successfully participating in the arts translates into teamwork, problem solving, creative thinking and business success.

We've organized this section around six key themes:

- Exuding Confidence
- Preparation Requires Discipline
- Team and Individual Settings
- Remain Calm and Improvise
- Clashing of Styles
- Dealing with a Difficult Person

We've written down our personal stories and our hope is that you can identify with some of these examples and even come up with a few of your own that you can then draw upon in your next interview or work situation. We all have experiences from our youth that have helped shape us. These are a few of ours.

Chapter 1: Exuding Confidence on Stage

If you survey most performers, several of them would say that they fear speaking and/or performing in front of people. This is what's called "stage fright" and it's common. In fact, a recent study conducted by Chapman University, listed public speaking/performing in front of an audience as one of people's top fears—*ahead* of death[i]. If you've ever felt this, don't worry, you're not alone. Performing, whether on your own or as part of a group, is an anxiety-producing situation, and even a seasoned veteran gets nervous at times and feels the pressure of being on stage. But every serious performer knows that at some point they must overcome this fear.

These same fears can manifest themselves in a business setting. However, every day people find the courage to break out of their comfort zones and speak up in meetings, give presentations, and get on stage to teach or give a speech.

Multiple techniques commonly learned in the arts can be used to combat this fear of performing in front of others, including: avoiding eye contact, pretending to not be on stage or the classic technique of visualizing that the audience is sitting in their underwear. These are all good techniques, but the most important is to exude confidence. You need to persuade the audience that you are in control of the situation and that you know what you are doing—even if there are more talented people in the room or subject matter experts watching your presentation. If you have ever heard the phrase "fake it 'till you make it," then you are aware of how valuable the skill of exuding confidence is, even if you aren't actually all that sure of yourself. By holding your head high, smiling, making eye contact and convincing yourself that "you've got this," the audience will pick up on your confidence, be more present, and give you the benefit of the doubt if anything sounds a bit off. Oftentimes they may also more polite and more supportive if you act confident.

The same is true in business situations. Whether you are giving a presentation to your boss or giving a speech in front of hundreds of colleagues, it is imperative that you exude confidence. This will give the impression that you are a trustworthy source of information. On the contrary, if you look nervous, uncomfortable or hesitant, skeptics and/or critics will "smell blood in the water," and rather than giving you the benefit of the doubt, they will seek to challenge and undermine you. Below are some case studies of how we learned as performing artists to get over our nerves and exude confidence even in the most vulnerable situations.

Overcoming Your Fear

As a concert pianist for over 10 years, Ruth Lee started taking lessons at the age of five. She had many teachers and performed on stage countless times, despite her hate and fear of performing in front of an audience. As the recital songs became more challenging, her fears and anxiety grew, which sometimes expressed itself through her body language and affected the mood of the audience.

To overcome this fear, she began to utilize a coping strategy, which was to pretend she was the only one in the room and free of distractions and the fear of a large crowd. By pretending she was just playing by herself, she could be more natural and confident in herself. This became easier for her over the years and she could control her outward nervousness and convince her audiences that she wasn't scared to be performing in front of them.

Ruth has used this experience in her professional career where she (as a co-owner and senior consultant at SBC) must give presentations to executive management teams fairly often. She still feels the same type of fear that she did when she played during recitals but she's applied those same coping mechanisms from her piano playing days to mask her nervousness.

Whether giving presentations in front of CEO's or her team, Ruth states that "people don't know that you are nervous unless you show it, so if you pretend and exude confidence, they will never know. If you are cool, calm and collected, it gives a different sense of the whole presentation than if you are fidgeting." It goes to show that her time playing piano taught her some very valuable lessons in overcoming fear in her work-life.

Smile and Make Eye Contact
Annie Thomas wasn't quite prepared for the type of stage performances she would give as a singer when she started out. A natural introvert, performing for a live audience was the last thing she had ever wanted to do. In fact, when she first started singing she would

often become sweaty and feel sick before performances. Initially, she was also a very rigid performer and people could tell that she dreaded being on stage.

Fond of the saying, "the show must go on," and after getting feedback from peers and family members, Annie started to come up with techniques to exude confidence and make it seem as if she was enjoying every minute of her performance (even if she wasn't). She used small tactics such as smiling, standing tall, using the stage as a prop and making eye contact with people she knew in the audience as a way to relax over time. These small changes all contributed to much better performances and helped her get through numerous vulnerable situations.

Annie still uses these strategies in her professional life. Although she currently doesn't do much public speaking, those select times where she has given presentations or when she's feeling uncomfortable at networking events, she falls back on those same strategies she used as a singer. When meeting people at conferences or professional events she still finds that flashing a smile at someone gives her a sense of confidence and it also helps make the other person feel more comfortable, which opens the door to a conversation. She continues to stand tall when presenting and talking to people, as this also helps her feel more confident and exudes interest whether it's a one-on-one conversation or a speech in front of a group.

Reminders for Exuding Confidence

1. Hold your head high, smile and make eye contact with each corner of the room.

2. Positive self-talk: This is a great way to help yourself feel more confident about the presentation or performance. Try telling yourself, "I'm going to rock this presentation!"

3. Visualize where you are most relaxed, happy and calm and then find a way to overlay that onto whatever situation you are in. This will help you squash your feelings of doubt.

4. Don't let on to your audience if you are nervous. Fake it until you make it!

5. Dress for success: Time after time, studies show that those who look the part feel more confident in themselves and will give off a sense of confidence and expertise to others around them.

Chapter 2: Preparation Requires Discipline

No matter what type of performing art you took on, you know that you can't just walk out onto a stage and succeed. If you have ever performed, you spent hours, days, weeks or even months preparing. Performing artists of all sorts know the process of preparation and importance of remaining disciplined in your practice. Hours spent preparing, whether for a group or solo performance can sometimes be grueling and I'm sure all of us remember a time when our parents bugged us to practice when we didn't want to. But what you learn is that you have to have self-discipline to practice even when you don't want to. It's not just talent— having the discipline to prepare is what leads to success whether you are the star performer, the backup or a member of the chorus.

Discipline comes from the willingness to work hard and put in the time and effort until it not only lives up to *your* standard, but to that of your peers, teacher or director as well. It is this determined attitude that sets you apart.

Preparedness isn't just about "getting it right." It is achieving a state of excellence where you prepare so much that your moves (if you are dancing) or notes (if playing the piano) are second nature and you will be focusing on playing to the audience rather than worrying about making a mistake. Malcolm Gladwell points out in his book *Outliers*, that for many people it may require up to 10,000 hours before mastery. Now, few of us have ever dedicated 10,000 hours to anything, and we're not saying this is a necessity, but you do need to be disciplined to master something.

Practice Makes Perfect

As someone who has been around music and performances her entire life and participated in her school band in middle school, Katie Thompson made sure to know the ins and outs of each song like the back of her hand. She remembers the hours of practice in school, on her own time and with other band members outside of class. Katie recalls days when she didn't want to put in the effort on her own part, but she knew that if she didn't prepare the best she could, the whole band would suffer.

She remembers a specific moment before a concert when her band director decided to change part of a song last minute so that another section of the band received more solo time. She was forced to then go home and learn those small changes the night before the performance. This last-minute change would've been easier for her to swallow at the time if the change had benefitted her section, but Katie recalls putting her head down, learning the new parts anyway, and watching those faces shine during the concert, knowing that her hard work was worth the result.

This type of discipline can serve you well throughout your career. None of us will ever have a job where we love what we do 100% of the time. There will be times when we must have the discipline to check, double check and re-verify our own work even when it is the last thing we want to do. And there will be times when you do all this work for the good of the group. It's in showing this discipline to practice or to go the extra mile when you don't want to, and doing it without someone to have to ask twice, that will separate you from co-workers and peers.

Always Expect the Unexpected
Rarely do things go 100% as planned in life. In fact, we're all faced with unexpected twists and turns whether it is in work or in life, yet thinking ahead and preparing for the unexpected is a valuable skill to mitigate risks

and the impact they may have on you personally or professionally. Kevin Wilhelm, CEO of SBC, learned the skill of "expecting the unexpected" at an early age.

Acting in his first major play at the age of 10, Kevin had over 500 lines in a Denison University production of *Waiting for Godot*, which was daunting because all the other actors were in college.

He recalled an evening when one of the cast members lost track of his lines and accidentally skipped ahead by 11 pages of the script. This left out several crucial plot elements for the audience and collectively he and the other actors had to figure out a way to bring this actor back to the correct spot in the script. Fortunately, the director had preached to all the cast members to prepare for every eventuality and "expect the unexpected," including what to do if the lights went out, someone forgot their lines or a key member never made it onto stage. Being a fifth grader who nobody really wanted to hang out with between scenes, Kevin got to know the other actors' entrances, exits and different stage cues. So, when this actor skipped ahead, Kevin fell back on his preparation and went off script to be able to steer the play back to where they needed to be to not only save the scene, but that night's performance for the entire audience.

Both case studies demonstrate how discipline and preparation allow you to lead, mitigate risk, and foster an environment of confidence for not only yourself but for that of others.

These are skills that are extremely valuable in a business setting. Whether you are meeting with a customer or another stakeholder, it's crucial to prepare for the unexpected. Kevin now preaches this in his office, so that if any staff member is giving a presentation they are always over prepared (we make sure we have backups in case the projector or laptop doesn't work, we always carry an extra clicker, batteries, etc.) because you never know how technology may fail you. More importantly, this skill has served our company well in preparing ahead of time for "what if" scenarios with clients:

- If a client or audience member continually interrupts with questions making it more difficult get our point across

- If the client hasn't read any of the pre-meeting materials
- If our time gets cut short due to weather or another meeting running over
- The questions we should expect and how to respond
- Worst case scenarios

All of these extra steps of preparation are just as important as the initial hours you put into a slide deck or report, because all of that can be sidetracked with a technology glitch or a person's intent of interrupting you. Therefore, by having the discipline to prepare for the unexpected, you'll be more confident for whatever situation you face.

Reminders for Preparation and Discipline

1. Sometimes you "just don't feel like practicing." Create a schedule of times to prepare during the week and stick to it. Schedule yourself enough time to prepare adequately.

2. Expect the unexpected. Create a list of all the things that could go wrong and prepare for them. This anticipation will enable you to handle them more professionally if/when they do come up.

3. If you're nervous or concerned, practice and put in the effort to get it right! There are no shortcuts.

4. If you're working on a team, being independently disciplined is crucial to your team's success. If you have a conflict that disables you from preparing adequately, communicate that to your team so they can cover.

Chapter 3: Working in Teams vs. Working Alone

At some point in their career, most performing artists have worked both alone and in teams. Some prefer one style over the other, but each requires a different mindset. Working with a team requires collaboration, cooperation, give and take, and learning to feed off one another's energy. Working alone requires learning how to own and dominate your individual performance on stage. Depending on your personality type and the type of performer you are, working in teams can sometimes be uncomfortable and more difficult if you prefer more of an individual style, and vice versa.

For example, if you have always been a solo musician and have to join a band or duo, this requires a totally different approach to practice, preparation and execution, because the end product depends not only upon how well you play, but how you play in combination with your band mates. On the flipside, if someone's only ever played in a band or ensemble, and is asked to play a solo, this requires a different mentality because there is nobody there to cover up a mistake or to provide energy to the audience if you don't bring it yourself.

The same is true in business. If you are used to working alone and never have to give or receive input or feedback from someone else, switching to a team oriented environment may be challenging. If you've only worked in a highly collaborative work environment where you've had people to proof your work and give suggestions for improvement, then being put on a task solo could create anxiety.

Understanding the differences and the ability to perform both as an individual, as well as part of a group is an essential skill. As more and more organizations shift to a collaborative work culture, with more team orientated projects (both in-person and virtually), the ability to deliver your best in a team environment is key.

Communication is Key

Performing in a large group has its challenges. As a key member of her school band, Katie had to take on numerous communication responsibilities in order for the band to play its best. As a percussionist, she recalls having to lead 40 different people and the challenge of trying to get everyone on the same page. This required collaboration and communication from all sides: the band director, each section of a band, and in her case, communication with just the other percussionists in her section. "It takes a ton of communication to deliver a final composition and we had to figure out how each instrument and section worked together, as well as learn non-verbal cues to signal to other sections when they should come in for each part of a song."

Katie recalls one concert where she and her band mates neglected to talk about a key moment in the song, the bridge. They were top-dog eighth graders—they didn't need to discuss those novice details. Turns out, their lack of communication beforehand about who entered when and at what volume caused a major mishap and a physical sounding dissonance that the audience definitely noticed. This could have been avoided had the percussionists communicated ahead of time, talked about the bridge and developed non-verbal cues prior to the performance. Had it been a solo trumpeter, the bridge could be whatever the musician wanted it to be; but in this case, the misstep in team communication meant a recognizable error that wouldn't be forgotten.

The same is true with business. We've all sat through group presentations whether it's in an office, at a conference or in the classroom and if the presenters are not on the same page, or if people talk out of order, the message gets lost because the audience begins to question the group's ability. The miscommunication by the group will be the thing that gets noticed and remembered no matter how good the content was. This is important because many companies are restructuring their internal foundations to mimic more of a team setting with many studies showing that Millennials prefer a collaborative work environment.[ii]

Finding Your Role within the Team
Kevin was in concert choir from 6th-12th grade and sang mostly as part of an ensemble, but also had numerous solos. Kevin had to learn how to tailor his voice, volume and energy differently between the two different roles. As part of a choir, Kevin learned that there were times when he needed to amplify his voice to cover for someone and at other times to tone it down and sing quieter to allow other voices to flourish. The song only worked for the audience if nobody stuck out (positively or negatively).

All of this has business application. There are times when someone forgets to say something during a presentation and you might have to speak up. There are times during a group presentation when you may need to add energy or tone it down and speak softer if that's what others are doing. As a CEO, Kevin is used to pitching and presenting to clients, but also knows when he needs to hand off the presentation to Ruth, Katie or Annie because they are the subject matter expert. And we all know the material and pay attention in case one of us leaves out a crucial point of information for a client, so that we can seamlessly include it. Moreover, each of us realizes that there are specific things that one of us needs to speak on and during that period the rest of us need to fade into the background. Before every presentation, we communicate our roles, the goal of the presentation, how it's going to be done and practice non-verbal cues if one of us needs to interrupt, add something or cut someone else off.

As the case studies above highlight, learning how to excel as an individual while working with and communicating as a team is an important work skill that can be learned through the performing arts at an early age.

Reminders for Working in Teams

1. Communicate ahead of time. In groups, talk and prepare for who is doing what, when and learn non-verbal cues.

2. Tailor your role within the team and how it fits into the overall final deliverable. There will be times when you are the leader and driver, and times when your role is more supportive.

3. Sometimes you'll need to speak louder or bring energy to a room to gain attention from the audience—never do this to outshine your teammates.

4. Recognize those times when you may need to soften your voice to be more in-line with your group so that the teams message isn't lost to the audience by one person

5. Make decisions as a team to allow for innovation, new ideas and to avoid conflict and animosity towards teammates.

Chapter 4: Remain Calm and Improvise

A performer very rarely makes it through a concert, play or performance without some type of mistake. While the audience may not realize that a mistake was made, an artist will always know when she/he has botched some part of their performance, no matter how insignificant it may be. The bigger skill is learning how to overcome the mistake, remain calm and not let the audience know. Of course, this is much easier said than done, especially if you have a Type A personality, but as a performer it's one of those skills you have to develop because you will likely make plenty of mistakes throughout your career.

The same is true in business. You will make mistakes in meetings or in front of audiences. Obviously, you try to avoid these, but when they do occur, what is most important is how you handle the situation. If it's a subtle mistake, chances are that while you notice it, only a few others will likely catch it—be calm, compose yourself, and carry on. If it is an obvious mistake, if you acknowledge it quickly, honestly, and with a sense of humor, your audience will be more forgiving and may forget about it quickly. Therefore, what's important is not that you never make a mistake in a front of others, it's how you compose yourself and handle it when you do.

Using Improv to Save the Day

Improv was an activity that Kevin stumbled upon in high school and college, but is one he attributes much of his business success to. Improv encourages thinking on your feet and trying out new ideas. It allows mistakes and teaches you how to quickly adapt from them when they do occur. While performing improv, Kevin learned different techniques to regain the audience if a sentence, line or comment fell flat. Improv is acting on a whim, with no rehearsed lines, so behind every interaction there is an element of fear and surprise as to where things are going to go next.

Kevin recalls a time during a performance where his partner on stage was taking the scene in one direction, and then said something so hilarious, that he couldn't help but laugh uncontrollably. He was laughing so much that he completely lost focus and forgot what his partner had just said. This gave way to some anxiety because he had no idea where to take the sketch next—not to mention that the audience was waiting for his next move.

While his mind was racing, he remembered his training and that it wasn't about making a mistake, instead, it was all about how one responded and recovered. Kevin then decided to go over the top with his laughing to a point that the audience though it was funny and started laughing with him. This provided Kevin with the time to come up with a few new lines to steer the sketch in a different direction, save the scene and keep the audience from turning on them.

Typically, during an improve sketch, the actors are expected to keep a scene going with no pauses, no matter what. So, in this situation rather than giving up, Kevin had to overcome his mistake, remain calm and figure out a reason for his uncontrolled laugh, and incorporate it into the sketch to make it seem planned all along.

According to Kevin, "Improv is one of the most important business skills you can learn. By being forced to think on your feet, you learn different ways to read people and how to adapt to any situation." There will no doubt be professional moments where you make a mistake or comment that you wish you could take back. Remember though that sometimes the only thing between success and embarrassment is how you handle the situation. This is where a performing arts skill can pay off dramatically (no pun intended) in the business world.

Learning to Think on Your Feet

As a singer, messing up on stage was terrifying for Annie. This was especially true as a soloist, which she was over two dozen times in her career. Like most performers, the more experienced she got the fewer mistakes she made, however, she learned early on that when you make a mistake, to save the day sometimes you must improvise.

One example was when she was singing at her cousins wedding for an audience of about 200 people. She started out great, but about two-thirds of the way through the song, she forgot an entire line. Earlier in her career, this would have side tracked her completely, but at this point, she had learned how to improvise.

She realized her mistake and felt extremely embarrassed but quickly thought on her feet and inserted random words while she sang until she could get back on track and remember the lyrics for the rest of the song. She did this so smoothly that the audience and her family members didn't even notice.

Annie has used this experience and others like it in her professional career. Now as a business professional, she attributes her ability to think on her feet and improvise from those techniques she learned in her singing career.

Reminders to Remain Calm and Improvise

1. Breathe and remain calm, avoid any type of indication that you have just made a mistake. The audience may not notice unless you clue them in.

2. Ad-lib or improvise when needed. Oftentimes this is the best savior for a mistake during a performance.

3. If it's appropriate, make a small joke regarding your mistake. In a business setting, this can lighten the mood in the room.

4. If something crucial is missed during a presentation DO NOT call out yours or a fellow colleague's mishap. Simply reiterate and apologize for leaving the information out.

5. Most importantly, realize that everyone makes mistakes more often than not—it's how you manage the mistake that either turns the audience for or against you.

Chapter 5: Dealing with the Inevitable "Clashing of Styles"

Anybody who's ever worked with other people knows the trials and tribulations of working with someone whose style is completely different from their own. This could be artistic style, work style, practicing habits, or any number of other things. Clashing styles, however, can create a chasm that may show up in the final performance and hurt your production. Therefore, getting on the same page with your partner(s) about your differing styles is a key to success for the overall vision of a performance, no matter the method of delivery.

Now this doesn't mean you have to be exactly the same, it just means that you have to communicate and be okay with your stylistic differences to make it work. Many bands break up not because they couldn't make great music but because eventually they couldn't get along in how they do things. To be successful in the delivery of any project, you need to be on the same page both stylistically and substantively. It is essential to acknowledge style differences and establish boundaries before you get to that key performance.

Learning to navigate the different styles and performing habits of others will also allow you to develop applicable skills for the business world, because it's very rare to find a job where everyone behaves the same way from the get go. By first recognizing different work styles and then establishing collective norms and habits, you will create better awareness and a mutual understanding of how each member of the team can best participate. You will also establish respect between team members which will lead to a stronger relationship between all working parties and a better end product.

Not Set Up for Success
Predominantly a country artist, Annie often found herself working with various audiences that didn't particularly like the genre of music she was used to singing. On occasion, she would let this criticism of her style get the best of her, but after a while she had to learn to have tough skin and be true to her artistic self.

This played out at one particular event where she was the opening act for a rock band in her hometown. As you can imagine, being from just outside a major metropolitan area, the audience was filled with mostly rock music fans that had little to no interest in country songs, and some even went so far as to completely leave the venue until her performance was over. It's never easy to witness someone walk out on your performance, but having this happen in your hometown was even more discouraging.

From the minute she was invited to open for this band, Annie wasn't set up for success—there was no communication or compromise for how varying their styles were. What she learned through this was to continue to be true to herself and to realize that not everyone is going to be a fan of your work, so she had to take this criticism constructively and look for opportunities to sing her music to audiences where the expectation was more in alignment than not.

Having audience awareness before you step on stage is crucial because, as you grasped from this example, no matter how well Annie sang, she was set up to fail from the start because she was signing country music to rock fans. The same is true in business—make sure your presentation is in alignment not only with what you and your team want to deliver, but in the format, language and expectation of your audience.

Taking the Time to Get on the Same Page
In a high school band (with the name Student Driver, I kid you not) Kevin learned an important lesson on stylistic clashes and the importance of everyone being truthful to who they were and expressing this up front. While auditioning for the annual Spring Gala, it became clear that there were different styles and personalities between the five-member band. Nobody could get on the same page in terms of music, energy (a more relaxed vs. high-energy performance style), volume (quiet vs. screaming rock) or the perception of their band they wanted to give.

Hours before the final audition the team was at wits end until one of the members finally asked, "What are we trying to accomplish here?" At that point each person got to say not only what part they wanted to play (lead singer, guitarist, bass, drummer, keyboard, etc.) but also how they wanted to play it. By taking the time to put all the cards on the table, the band was able to come together. They were able to understand what each of them brought to the band in terms of style and how to best maximize each person's talent and what they wanted to do. This enabled Student Driver to choose the three songs that balanced out each individual style and allowed each of the members to shine and play to their strengths—and it worked out for them since the band was chosen to play at Homecoming the next fall.

Clashing Styles at Work

When SBC was a younger company, we always asked about work style and environment in interviews and every candidate said that they were okay working in "a fast-paced, energetic work environment." The reality though, was that some of the more thoughtful, introverted individuals really struggled with this work style and were just not set up for success from the beginning. Therefore, we had to move desks around and place "the talkers" next to each other, so that the introverts had their space and the extroverts had theirs.

We're certainly not saying it's bad to have different styles – in fact, we encourage diversity. The point is to be open and upfront about the situation in order to take the necessary steps to maximize the strengths of the team.

Reminders for Reconciling Clashing Styles

1. Have open communication about work styles, norms and goals.

2. Be aware and understanding of someone else's style and figure out how best to complement one another and maximize each other's strengths.

3. To avoid conflict, try switching up habits from time to time so everyone feels as if their work norm is being appreciated.

4. Be true to yourself, but realize sometimes we might all need to adjust our styles for the greater good.

5. Realize that some time you may be set up for failure from the beginning in terms of style. Make sure you find an environment that will enable you to succeed.

Chapter 6: Dealing with a Difficult Person

Working with a difficult cast or ensemble member can be a big hurdle to overcome for any artist. Dealing with difficult team members doesn't stop at the peer level either. Directors and conductors can bring their own elements of personality and ego that make things more difficult and dramatic then they need to be. Every performer (no matter the age or level) has dealt with someone that's been just plain challenging, but learning how to work with this person while simultaneously bringing the best out of oneself is crucial. This can be tricky but it's best to handle this at the first sign of trouble with a teammate so that you can to get to the bottom of the issue, solve it and find harmony. That way everyone can be focused on the job at hand and not the interpersonal conflict amongst teammates.

The skills developed when dealing with a difficult teammate, cast member or band mate will also come in handy later in life when you are dealing with a problematic co-worker.

Dealing with a Difficult Instructor, Manager or Boss

Over the span of her 14 years as a concert pianist, Ruth had many instructors—some of whom she loved, but many who were difficult to get along with because of their utilitarian approach to teaching. Ruth recalls one teacher in particular, who she just did not jive with at all.

The teacher expected long hours of practice and focused the direction of the lessons on classical pieces and technicalities, leading to the two of them often butting heads over very small things—even how long her fingernails were. This instructor went so far as to passive aggressively set clippers next to the piano in order to urge Ruth to cut her nails. This difference caused major tension and unrest at both lessons and recitals.

This effected Ruth's interest in playing and her commitment to the long hours of practice that her instructor desired. Finally, after months of dancing around their issues, Ruth struck up the courage to talk to her teacher, whom she viewed as an elder, and explain why her heart wasn't in it anymore.

While this wasn't what her instructor wanted to hear, the instructor realized that she would lose Ruth's talents if they couldn't find a compromise and started to let her choose songs that were more fun and eased up on the criticism of the little things. Although her teacher was extremely difficult to work with, Ruth decided that talking to her about these issues directly and working to solve them enabled their relationship to improve (which had a positive effect on Ruth's motivation to continue playing).

While it was a tough situation to work through, Ruth has applied these learnings to her professional career when she works with difficult clients or co-workers. She's learned that one of the most important tactics is to openly communicate and to explain the "why" behind disagreements. This has helped her when she knows what she is doing is right, but receives pushback from someone who is difficult to work with.

Working with Unreliable Teammates

As a Thespian, Kevin has many stories detailing his experiences with difficult cast members. One of the most poignant is a story where a fellow actor who played a key character decided that he was not going to come out on stage that night, just because he was ticked off about something the director had said to him. While the rest of the cast, both on and off stage, was waiting for this person to come on stage, Kevin was frantically searching his brain for an escape route. Luckily, because he and a few friends thought that this actor might just pull this type of stunt, Kevin had memorized just enough of the actor's lines to spontaneously play both roles.

That cast mate who decided to put his ego and feelings above all else is a great example of someone who is not only hard to work with, but untrustworthy. Kevin learned from those incredibly stressful two minutes on stage that sometimes you have to be prepared for people to simply let you down, and be ready to carry on in case they do.

The same is true for business. You may have co-workers who don't live up to expectations or slack on projects. Sometimes to survive in the business world, you must realize a co-worker is unreliable, and that if you can only count on them 75% of the time, you are better off finding someone else to do the job and keep moving forward.

While the popular belief is that performing arts is "just for fun," it truly can teach transferable skills to better handle conflict in the business world. Those classic "tell me about a time" interview questions can sometimes be best answered from experiences as a performing artist, rather than only drawing upon professional experiences.

Reminders for How to Work with a Difficult Person

1. If it's a difficult colleague or peer, try and get to the root cause of the problem and understand "the "why" behind the conflict.

2. If they are an instructor/manager, be sure to be true to yourself and explain what isn't working.

3. Realize that if a co-worker is unreliable and untrustworthy, sometimes you just have to move on and find a way to work around them.

Section Two: How Playing Sports Can Positively Impact Your Business Career

Sports can teach us many things that translate into other parts of our lives. They teach us about hard work, leadership, grit and numerous other traits and skills. Team sports instill the importance of being able to work effectively with others towards a common goal, while individual sports teach us about drive, perseverance, and the discipline to perfect your craft. Therefore, whether you were a star athlete or someone who simply played for fun, this section of the book is designed to demonstrate to you that the skills and attributes that you have learned from sports can translate into your next interview, job, or career.

Think back to a time where you had to compete for a spot on a team. Were you nervous? Did you practice extra hard so that you made the team to avoid being cut? The memory of the determination you showed then is something to reflect and draw upon now in situations when you face a difficult task in the workplace. Moreover, the benefits of playing sports have been shown to increase confidence in individuals and help them build intangible skills often not taught in a traditional classroom.

In fact, a recent study published in the *Journal of Leadership and Organizational Studies* found that of all high school students in the US that played sports, 43% tended to have better leadership skills and had higher levels of self-respect & confidence[iii]. Those benefits pay off in the professional world whether you played basketball, soccer, volleyball, baseball, tennis or whatever sport it may have been.

Below are real life stories from the SBC team (Annie, Katie, Kevin and Ruth), their involvement in sports through high school and college and how these experiences helped shape their professional careers today. In fact, the company attributes some of its effectiveness to the fact that all of the employees have learned teamwork and other intangible skills having played sports.

The following case studies, just like in the arts section, are designed to showcase how the characteristics learned from playing sports correlate to success in the business world. In addition, we want readers to relate to these stories, recognize their own skills from their own experiences, articulate them in interviews and apply them to their work lives.

While a very small percentage of athletes actually turn pro in the sport they played, eventually all adults "go pro" as they choose a profession that will pay their bills. Therefore, a strong argument can be made that athletics helps prepare individuals for success in the business world.

We've organized this section around five key themes:
- Leadership
- Strategy, Anticipation and Preparation
- Knowing Your Role
- Learning to Make Mistakes
- Grit

Chapter 7: Leadership

Playing any type of team sport teaches you about leadership. You also get exposed to different types of leaders—those that lead by example, inspirational leaders who encourage others and leaders who motivate by yelling and instilling fear. Through team sports you learn how to interact, motivate, build relationships and work towards a common goal—whether you were appointed as a captain, took on a leadership role, or were just a good teammate who followed others. Because sports can often provide a competitive, fast-paced environment similar to the business world or start-up sector, being an athlete gives you experience that you can draw on throughout your professional career.

Finding Your Leadership Style
Annie nurtured her leadership skills through her years of playing soccer by seeing how crucial it was to provide a great example for other players to follow. Leading others wasn't something that she had been good at in other parts of her life, but as she got older and more involved in her sports teams, she took it upon herself to set the expectation for work ethic and effort.

Annie was voted a captain of her soccer team during her junior year at Seattle Pacific University (SPU) which had been a goal of hers since she first began the recruiting process. Early on in her captaincy, her coach encouraged her to be a more vocal leader, which wasn't really her style or something that she felt genuine in doing. Consequently, as the year went on and she began to grow more comfortable in her role, she made a choice to stick with her more reserved, "lead by example" style.

This not only fit her personality better, but since her co-captain was more of a vocal leader, this enabled Annie to appeal to those players on the team who didn't respond well to the yelling, intense type of leadership. Despite there being constant pushback from her coach about speaking up more, Annie knew that her words of encouragements meant more to her players when they came from a genuine place rather than a forced one. Annie received great affirmation from her teammates about her leadership method throughout her year and a half as a captain.

When you get into difficult team situations in the workplace or other elements of your life, knowing what type of leader you are and acting in a way that is true to yourself is extremely beneficial and will help you be a better leader. Establishing your leadership style and communicating it early on will help others understand your methods, help to avoid conflict and may even be more effective at motivating others than following someone else's style.

As a newer member of the SBC team, Annie still tends to be more reserved and quiet and while she's not currently in a leadership position, she continues to lead by example when it gets hectic in the office or when someone needs to be reminded to take a deep breath and sets the expectation to others of staying late until the job is done.

Learning How to Lead Different People
Much of Kevin's role as CEO is about leading, inspiring and helping his co-workers and students play to their strengths and realize their potential. He first found his voice as a leader while playing sports, mostly through soccer.

Kevin was one of the better players on his soccer team in high school but never the best. While some athletes get chosen to be the captain because of their talent, Kevin was always chosen because of his leadership skills and ability to motivate his teammates. It was here where he learned the need to use different leadership styles when motivating others, something that he still relies on today, professionally.

For example, Kevin realized that for some of his teammates, he simply needed to lead by example. He would show up early, always hustle and give his 100% on the field. He didn't need to yell at most people, he just needed to set the tone for others to follow. This approach worked for most but not all of his teammates, as some needed to be nurtured, supported and encouraged (especially if they made a mistake), while a few occasionally needed a good talking to in order to light a fire in their belly. He had to know how each teammate reacted best and tailor his leadership style to each individual in order to get the best play and effort out of them.

Kevin brought this skill to his professional career as he's had to adapt to different employees based upon their learning styles, values and motivational triggers. He's found that after managing over 100 people in the last 10 years, that most of his co-workers feed off of being led by example, while some need to be shown what to do, encouraged and supported. But for three former employees who viewed his empathy as a weakness, he had to use a much more straight forward and blunt approach when their work product was unacceptable.

The fact is, he never would have been a successful manager or leader had he not been forced to learn various leadership and motivational styles from his sports background and how to get the best out of each individual.

Leading Through Empathy
Katie, an associate at SBC, spent most of her athletic years as co-captain of both her club and high school volleyball teams where she led with confidence and upheld the teams' mental and emotional stability. At the end of her playing career, she was recruited to coach a 14-year-old club team and had to learn a whole new type of leadership style: coaching.

She had to draw upon both her own experiences with her high school coach (who showed unprecedented devotion to the team) and that of a new type of empathetic leadership she wanted to exemplify to this U14's team. She understood that these girls were freshmen in high school and were going through a lot of changes in their life. Volleyball was just one piece of their lives that they were trying to find their identity in.

Knowing that a coach can have a significant impact on a player, Katie understood that her leadership style as coach was going to be very different than that of a fellow captain. This required a layer of deep mentorship that showed empathy and understanding, while also setting appropriate expectations and pushing them to be better players.

Through this experience, Katie learned how to effectively manage a team by understanding her role as both leader and mentor, and taking deep concern in the personal development of her players. In today's athletic environment where so much emphasis is placed on winning by coaches and parents alike, Katie believed that delivering results was only half of her job, and found it just as rewarding to also attend to the emotional and mental stability of the whole person. Not surprisingly, this approach led to her team winning tournaments while also building up strong individuals to face much greater challenges than just volleyball.

Reminders about Leadership

1. Sports put you in a fast paced, ever changing, competitive environment, so the leadership experience you gain in sports is applicable in business or a start-up environment as well.

2. It's important to be true to who you are and lead in the manner that you are most comfortable.

3. Leadership takes many different forms – some lead by example, others motivate verbally, while others sit back and observe. All are valid methods and various forms may be needed at different times. People need different types of leadership and it's important to know when to provide which kind.

4. Organizational leadership requires delegation.

5. Not everyone responds to the same leadership style. Effective leaders tailor their message and style to the people they are trying to lead to what works best for those individuals.

6. Leadership involves empathy and can sometimes mean caring more about the individual you are leading than the immediate goal in the short-term.

Chapter 8: The Importance of Strategy, Anticipation and Preparation

Sports can be brutally unpredictable and you have to be able to anticipate the next play, respond to your opponent's game plan, and develop a strategy that gives your team the best chance for success. The same is true in business, as things never play out exactly as planned, so you must prepare for multiple scenarios. For example, in sports, what happens if your star player gets hurt the day before the game? Do you have a backup plan? In business, what is your plan for if/when things get derailed?

Just like you might have anticipated an opponent's likeliest and best moves in sports, if you can do this in the business world your chances of success are much greater. Whether it is giving a presentation or meeting with a client or colleague, try to understand each person's perspective and respective tendencies ahead of time and plan for it.

Prepare beforehand and ask yourself, "Who are the skeptics, what will people potentially react negatively to, and what is the best way to tailor your message and engage people positively about what they care about." Also, think about what could go wrong from the technical perspective (the PowerPoint doesn't work, the mic doesn't work, no projector, etc.) because if you have a strategy that prepares you for all of these things, you will feel much less stress and be able to move forward more successfully when surprises come your way.

Sailing as a Metaphor

Many people think of sailing as a hobby, but it's not, it is a sport that involves hundreds of intricacies that are needed to be successful in a race. Most critically, you must be able to chart a course and then be able to navigate to it. Kevin is fond of saying, "You don't know where you are going, unless you know where you are." This is true in sailing because you can't plot your course unless you know exactly where you are starting from.

This is actually a great metaphor for business, too. If you are trying to come up with a new strategy, whether it's marketing, product sales, growth, etc. the first thing you must do is assess where you are. You can't just set a goal and start implementing a strategy—your coordinates could be off or you may be doing things out of order that will derail you from success. Therefore, just like in sailing, when implementing a new business strategy, first understand where you are, set your compass point as to where you are going, and map your strategy back from there in order to achieve it.

Always Thinking Ahead

Playing tennis entails strategizing about each hit and reacting to your opponent's every movement and level of play. As a singles player for many years, Ruth Lee had become excellent at reading the game and responding to the other player's swing, expressions, movements and abilities. For each section of the court, depending on where the player was standing, Ruth learned how to hit the ball in a difficult spot for her opponent to reach. "If they are in the back court, I'm going to hit it close to the net. If they are close to the net, I'll slam it in the back. Sometimes if I've noticed they're not good at running full court, I'll put spin on my shot so they can't get to it at all." This anticipation and response to the other person's actions helped her to win many matches. Not only did she have to strategize in the middle of a match, she had to be able to anticipate the other player's reactions and return shots as well.

In her professional role as a senior consultant at SBC, she continues to apply these skills. Ruth makes executive presentations, conducts meetings and responds to clients' needs all the time, and therefore has learned to utilize this skill to anticipate questions and prepare her strategy for who will be in the room.

Just like in sports, where you may prepare more diligently for a highly-ranked player versus a junior varsity caliber player, the same is true when preparing to meet with an Executive or CEO. She knows the importance of always thinking ahead and anticipating the type of questions to expect based upon the person she is dealing with. She has mentored others and passed this motto down to her co-workers as always being one step ahead has proved successful for her.

Prepare for Your Time to Come

Another one of Kevin's favorite phrases is that, "it's all in the preparation." Many people think Kevin is just a natural facilitator and that he can just "ad lib" in a meeting at a moment's notice. The truth is that Kevin prepares diligently before every meeting, preparing for all scenarios—something that was drilled into his head by his rugby coach in college.

Kevin joined the rugby team as a sophomore in college. He actually had no intention of ever joining the rugby team, but his friend said the team would be a player short the next day and just needed a body. Needless to say, his first game didn't go well. He didn't know his team's strategy, how to read the defense, what he should do or where to place himself on the field in certain situations. Compounding this was that he was also one of the smallest players on the field; so needless to say, he got tossed around like a rag doll and pretty beat up. Not wanting to repeat this mentally or physically, and wanting to be the best teammate he could be, Kevin met with the coach often those first couple of weeks and became a quick study.

Kevin was a fly half (which is the football equivalent of the running back), who is the first to receive the ball from the scrum half (quarterback equivalent) after they pull it from the scrum (the big mess of 7 people on each side crashing into each other). In this role, once Kevin received the ball, he could run forward (and get tackled by a bunch of huge dudes), kick the ball in the air and try and run under it, or he could lateral the ball to his teammates for them to run and then drop back into position.

Kevin knew he didn't have the size or experience to excel unless he prepared vigorously. He worked closely with the coach to understand the best play depending upon field position, opponent formation, opponent tendency and score in the game. He learned to read the opposition and adjust his team's strategy on a dime, constantly making adjustments based on field position, alignment and the momentum of the play. This took him from a clueless rookie to a contributing member of the team in a few short weeks.

This played out somewhat similarly for Kevin professionally when he first moved to Seattle and was trying to break into the sustainability scene. He didn't know anyone, didn't have any local clients and was often the youngest person in the room. Having been a successful consultant in Michigan in the years prior, Kevin knew he had the skills but was a little hesitant to practice his trade in the much bigger and greener city of Seattle where so many more established professionals in the field already existed.

So, what did Kevin do? He prepared for the competitive sustainability industry in Seattle. He kept attending conferences, learned who was who, went to networking events and joined the Sustainability Committee at the Seattle Chamber of Commerce, where he often sat in the row behind the main table because he didn't have much to offer up those first nine months. About one year in, the committee realized that it needed some research done on a proposed Renewable Portfolio Standard (RPS) for the State of Washington.

Being a sustainability guru, Kevin had been following this issue vigorously and he volunteered to write a white paper and present it to the rest of the committee. In addition to an analysis of both the pros and cons of the initiative, he wanted to make sure the committee was prepared for where the opposition may come from, what their issues might be, and how to best alleviate their concerns while pushing the issue forward.

His diligence and preparation allowed him to become the point person on a hot topic and establish his credentials with that group and its two co-chairs. Now many years have passed and Kevin is considered a thought leader and one of the "go-to" experts in this field, all from being ready for his time.

If You Put In the Prep, the Score Will Take Care Of Itself

Famous basketball coach John Wooden once said, "The score will take care of itself if you put in the effort." Playing competitive soccer for most of her life, Annie knows that the correct preparation before a game can make a huge difference in the outcome. She recalls a specific game from the Sweet 16 of the NCAA Tournament where her SPU her team was playing a school from California that not only had a much better record than SPU, but was just an all-around higher-caliber team.

Their opponent was very successful at set pieces (corner kicks, free kicks, etc.) so her team put in a lot of additional practice time to defend all types of these set pieces in the week prior to playing them. When the game occurred, SPU ended up defending twice as many corners as they took, but never relented. Despite being the underdog, Annie's team actually won the game and attributes it to putting in the extra time and effort to counter their strengths during practice the week before.

For Annie, preparation in the consulting world is very similar—this was especially true when she was first getting started. If she knew that she lacked a certain level of expertise for the client's industry, it was crucial to over prepare and to put in the extra effort to know as much about the client, their needs, industry nuances and the people that she would be meeting with ahead of time. This kind of preparation can go a long way to make up for a lack of experience.

Reminders about the Importance of Strategy, Anticipation and Preparation

1. Expect the unexpected.

2. It's all in the preparation. If you have a strategy with a backup plan, you can better adjust on the fly or when adversity strikes. Failing to prepare can lead to stress and a lesser performance, there is no excuse for not being prepared.

3. Know your audience. Try and anticipate their questions, concerns and issues before you step into a meeting or give a presentation.

4. You don't know where you are going until you know where you are. Assess your position first before creating a strategy forward.

5. To beat a tougher opponent, there is no short cut to putting in the hard work and extra time.

6. You will face headwinds; sometimes all it takes is a simple jive or a tack to get the wind to start working for you as opposed to against you.

7. Sometimes preparation and anticipation can overcome skill and experience. Prepare vigorously for your time to come, so when the opportunity does present itself, you are ready to seize it.

8. If you are young and you are meeting with someone older or more experienced, one way to level the playing field is to over prepare and know everything about the organization, individuals and industry before walking through the door.

Chapter 9: Knowing Your Role

In athletics, oftentimes your role will be different depending on the needs of your team, the coach or your skill set. All athletes at one time or another had a circumstance where they maybe didn't get to play the position they wanted to or get the amount of playing time they thought they deserved. This could be because there was an upper classman in front of you or someone who played that position better, or maybe your skills were needed in a different position because that is what the team needed. Or maybe your role changed quite suddenly due to an injury or illness. These are all examples where one's role may not be what someone thought it should be.

If you are a soccer player and your primary strength is your speed, then it would make sense to play as a striker. But if there already is a great goal scorer up top who is more adept at finishing shots than you, then maybe you should be positioned as an outside halfback or winger. If you are a volleyball player and are extremely athletic, but your team already has a libero, then maybe it would be beneficial to your team if you were a setter where you can use your agility to set up great plays on offense.

This gets to the importance of knowing one's role. No matter where you end up playing on a team, clear communication about your role, why you are playing there and how this benefits the team overall is essential to the success of your team.

If you listen to any pro football analyst, whether they are on ESPN or sports radio, when they talk about a team's success, they typically come back to the fact that the coach has explained to each player what their role is. Everyone knows what is expected of them, what they should focus on, what they will be called upon to do, and what they are expected _not_ to do.

This helps keep animosity out of the locker room by players understanding why they are getting the playing time they are (even if they think they should be getting more), as well as clarifying whom should be taking on specific tasks so that when the pressure is on at the end of the game, the right player ends up with the ball in her hands and not everyone is trying to play hero.

The same is true at work. When employees are unclear as to what they should focus on, or if you have a situation where roles have been left vague or split between two different people, that is where confusion sets in and neither the individual, nor the organization is functioning at an optimal level.

The Importance of Knowing Your Role
In one of Kevin's previous jobs, his boss would ask to meet with him and his co-worker and say that she wanted a quick, small task done, and then she would walk out and leave it up to the two of them to figure it out. Both would talk, and be unsure about who was to take the lead. Typically, neither person had much extra time because they already had too much on their plates. Also, because both people were given the task, neither really felt ownership and hoped the other would do it. When it came time to present to their boss, both Kevin and his co-worker had a ton of excuses as to why the task didn't get done. However, the true reason was because the manager hadn't been clear as to each person's role or how the task should get broken down between the two.

It's just like in sports where you may have four running backs on a football team and each one believes that they should be the "short yardage, touchdown back." If this is the case and each of the four thinks *they* should be the one getting the ball, then whoever the coaches choose will leave the other three wondering why they didn't get the carry and possibly even interrupting the play. Moreover, it's likely that the three that didn't get the carry will start to question the coach's decisions and feel slighted, whether the team scores or not. Clarity in communicating each person's role, whether in sports or business, lessens confusion and anxiety, gives each individual confidence in their task and gives your team a better chance to achieve its goals.

From Captain to Injured Contributor
As mentioned earlier, Annie was named captain of the SPU soccer team during her junior year. This was a huge honor and something she took extremely seriously because she knew that in this role, she was someone that the players looked to for motivation and someone the coaches looked to for leadership.

She had always led on the field by setting a great example, but all of that changed when, during a regular season game, she felt a sharp pain in her right knee and had to be taken off the field. She had battled knee injuries throughout her career but after multiple doctors looked at it, she found out that she had an irreversible hole in her cartilage, would need surgery, and that her body simply had had enough. This was devastating to her not only because it meant an end to her college playing career and the sport she loved, but also because she felt like she couldn't be there for the team in her captain role when they needed her.

In just one day, she went from leading the team on the field to having to play the awkward role of bench captain. This role change took her a long time to figure out because she had to learn how to lead and motivate without directly being involved in the field of play. Her tactics and approach to relationship building and communication had to change to a more observatory and strategic role.

She had to learn how to use her strengths elsewhere and, although devastated, Annie felt that she was a part of something bigger and realized that her teammates still looked up to her even if she wasn't on the field with them.

In business, there will be times where your role changes. This can be for better or for worse, and can happen over time or in an instant. In

Annie's case, being named captain was like a promotion, but when she got injured it felt just like a demotion. In each case, she had to learn to adapt her skills, mindset and role to what was needed. Her ability to accept the reality of her role change has paid off professionally because as SBC has grown, she has taken on new responsibilities and expectations—even the type of work has shifted as company needs have evolved.

Therefore, whatever your role within a company may be, it's important to know it well, embrace it, be flexible and understand how the tasks and responsibilities play into the bigger context of the organization.

Embracing a Leadership Role Not Because You Want To, But Because You Should
Playing tennis throughout her entire high school career, Ruth recalled her role shifting to that of a leader not because she wanted to, but because that was what the team needed. At the time, she wasn't the captain and some of the other women on the team were stronger players, but there was a void in leadership and nobody else was stepping up. As an older player with more years of experience, she knew

she had to step into this role because the younger players weren't going to.

Despite not being an all-star player, Ruth grew into her leadership role and became more comfortable not only mentoring the younger players, but also competing with the other more skilled players. "Being in that leadership role was great—to teach and coach other players who were just learning to love the sport was awesome and a great learning experience for me," said Ruth. "It also helped me grow and realize that sometimes your role is bigger than what you thought it would be—or even should be."

Ruth's embrace of this leadership role through tennis instilled in her the tools and confidence to take on a larger role at work when it was required. As more of a quiet leader who prefers to lead by example, she has had to take on various roles with clients as project manager and internally directing colleagues under her all the time. Learning to motivate, coach and mentor others is typically a role that older individuals with more seniority take on, but just as she learned through tennis, she's been able to step into the role and succeed.

Being a Team Player

Entering high school as an outside hitter (a front row attacker) for her high school, Katie knew her role was going to have to change. She was competing for playing time against two teammates for the same position who were taller, had higher verticals than her, and had been playing volleyball since they could walk.

Soon after making the varsity team, Katie began to train as a libero (the back row defensive specialist in the different colored jersey) because that was the position that her team needed, after losing an all-state player. The mentality, movements, and agility required to play this role were so different from what Katie had been training for the previous four years. She went from having to be an offensive powerhouse to the one that had to absorb those hard spikes and anticipate those smart tips. She also went from being one of the players on the court that received all of the glory for hitting the finishing slam to someone now stuck in the back only making digs, sets and plays to keep the point alive.

At first it was difficult for her to not want to call for back row offensive plays and she often made errors early on in this transition, because her mindset was still focused on the offensive move at the end of the play rather than the perfect pass she had to make first in her new role. After a few weeks of training and time spent with the coach and key players, Katie began to take ownership of her role and learn that the glory and applause the fans provided for those spikes, kills, and offensive move were only possible because of a strong defensive player setting the stage for the set and attack.

Through this experience, Katie learned the significance of understanding one's role fully. She's applied that in her professional career as well, realizing that not everyone gets time on stage or face time with a client, but that sometimes the most important people on a team are the ones behind the scenes who rarely get the glory.

Reminders about Knowing Your Role

1. The best teams function when everyone's role is clear. Establish roles early on so that there is no confusion.

2. Clear communication on roles can help alleviate anxiety, jealousy and concern from teammates ahead of time.

3. One's role can change in an instant, which can lead to confusion. To get over this, one must understand what is required in a new role and why. Being able to be flexible in the short term or in a pinch is important.

4. When a role changes, your mindset about the person you are doesn't have to change, but it may just manifest itself differently. This doesn't mean you skills or talents have been lost, but rather, they are just being utilized differently.

5. Sometimes you must embrace a leadership role, even if you don't want to or don't have the confidence to do so. If that is what is required by your team, sometimes you must step up for the greater good.

6. Sometimes the most important people on a team are the ones behind the scenes who rarely get the glory.

Chapter 10: Learning to Make Mistakes

You have to learn to bounce back from mistakes and failure when you play sports, or else everyone would just give up. Whether it's in practice or you miss the potential winning shot at the end of a big game, the ability to make mistakes and then learn from them is essential. Nobody ever got to be where they are without first missing thousands of shots whether it be in basketball, soccer, or a quarterback missing thousands of throws in football. Even the greatest hitters in baseball who hit close to .400, miss six out of every ten times.

Sometimes our best learning happens through failure because this allows you to diagnose what went wrong, why and what to do differently the next time around. Plus, unless you are a professional athlete, the stakes are never truly that high compared to other things in your life, so being able to learn the process of making mistakes and correcting them is an important skill.

The business world is similar in that you aren't going to know everything on your first day. At some point, you are going to make a mistake and someone will catch it, whether it's a co-worker, a boss or client. The more important thing is to use those skills you learned through sports to first admit the error, diagnose what went wrong, correct it, and then learn from it so that it doesn't happen again.

The reason we bring this up is that some people can get hung up on perfection or become so risk adverse that they don't take risks that could help them learn, grow and advance their career. Don't get us wrong, we're not saying "don't worry, make mistakes, there are no consequences." It's just the opposite. The following stories are meant to convey that mistakes made while playing sports teach us how to recover from failure that is relevant in our daily professional lives.

Learning from Failure
This may seem counter-intuitive in the business world, where books are written about success, not failure, but the reality is that none of these business leaders got to be where they are without first failing a few times. Over the years, many people have asked Kevin, "What has

been the key to your success?" His response is perseverance and the importance of learning from one's failures. That isn't exactly Forbes Best Seller List material, but this is true. What Kevin learned by failing in sports has been key to shaping him into who he is today.

Kevin's athletic career in high school and college was full of mixed results. In fact, he was once cut from his 9th grade basketball team, even though in the previous two years his team had only won a total of one game.

However, it was in college, when Kevin was a three-sport athlete that he truly learned the importance of learning to fail. A collegiate diver his sophomore year, Kevin was always more comfortable to attempt dives that he already knew, because his chances of ending up in a painful back smack was much less. Just like in business, for many people it is easier and more comfortable to continue doing what you are doing well, instead of being pushed into something new.

Kevin's coach insisted to him that he would never improve unless he pushed himself out of his comfort zone, so he forced him to attempt new dives, often off the high-dive before he felt ready. Kevin realized that you don't learn from your successes nearly as much as you do your failures, because once you smack your back a few times from 15 feet up in the air, you learn to adjust quickly. He learned different nuances that eventually made him a much stronger diver and his scores improved. Kevin learned what NOT to do a lot quicker from a few failures than he would have otherwise.

The same is true with business. Innovation, creativity, and new ideas often come from being willing to try new things and failing a few times before you come up with the right solution. SBC strives for excellence in all they do and 100% customer satisfaction, but they realize that when piloting a new product or service, you aren't going to get things perfect right out of the box.

They learn from the moments when aspects don't turn out like they thought they would, or when the customer reacts differently than expected, or even when the process wasn't as smooth as they were hoping for. These small lessons help to improve the product each time, so that when they get ready to unveil it for prime time, all the bugs have been ironed out.

This ability to embrace learning from failure that Kevin had first experience in diving has enabled his firm to remain agile, innovative, and quick to respond to market demand, while also looking for ways for continuous improvement.

Practice *IS* the Time for Mistakes
As mentioned earlier, Ruth was an avid tennis player, but like many high school athletes, she was reluctant to practice the weakest elements of her game in front of her peers for fear of making mistakes in front of them. She realized though that if she never worked on these, her opponent would try to exploit her weaknesses, just as she would theirs. Therefore, she decided that, despite her fear of embarrassing herself in front of others, she would work on her weak spots (backhand, net play, etc.) to improve and to set an example for underclassmen that it was okay to make mistakes, and that practice was the perfect place to do that.

To overcome her weakness at the net, Ruth would practice tirelessly on her own playing close to the net. At first it was frustrating because she made many errors, but after weeks of practicing, she began to feel comfortable at the net and even began to play there in her matches. Soon enough, she was as good at the net as she was in the back court. She realized that to be a well-rounded tennis player, she needed to acknowledge and address her weaknesses head on, rather than trying to avoid them.

Similarly, in business, Ruth wasn't fond of public speaking or giving presentations in front of a large crowd. She often worried about saying the wrong thing, not being able to answer questions or just freezing up completely. Knowing this was a weakness and that as her role grew and evolved that she was going to be giving important presentations, she realized that she needed to deploy that same work ethic and practice on her speaking just as she did her net play in tennis. She practices vigorously before each presentation and is willing to make mistakes in front of her co-workers so that when it's time to present to a client, she's ready.

Fear of failure is a powerful emotion, especially in a professional setting. However, without taking some risks and being willing to make mistakes during practice, you will stagnate and never realize your full potential. In the wise words of Babe Ruth, "Never let the fear of striking out keep you from playing the game."

Using Failure as Motivation
As a participant on his University's boxing team, one of the most important lessons Kevin Merrill (a former intern of SBC) learned was how to recover from failure. "If you get knocked down in the ring, how you chose to react to that situation dictates your future success not only in boxing but also in life." He recalls learning this lesson firsthand when he traveled to Reno, Nevada for his first ever boxing fight in 2015. He felt very confident going into the fight because he had been training for months and his coaches assured him that he was more than ready.

Unfortunately, the fight didn't go as anyone had hoped and he ended up getting knocked out in the first round. This defeat was unexpected, demoralizing, and borderline embarrassing for him. He even sustained a serious concussion and couldn't box again for weeks. During that time, he remembers considering quitting the sport multiple times, which would have been understandable but he also felt that would be the easy way out.

Instead, he decided to use the experience as motivation to train harder and make sure that he was never knocked out again. Within a few months, Kevin was back in the ring and winning fights. By the end of the year he was elected President of the team—and no one would have guessed that he had considered quitting just months before. Learning to look at failures as an opportunity for growth and motivation rather than disappointments was a pivotal point in his boxing career and a lesson he draws on to this day.

This kind of reaction to failure is one that most employers looks for in their workers today. Mistakes will happen, but it's the reaction to these errors that is an indicator of strong character and the willingness to improve. As Kevin Merrill showed, "It's not about getting knocked down; it literally is about how you get up!"

<u>Failing on Day One</u>
The very first time Katie truly played volleyball (beyond just bumping a foam ball back and forth in gym class) was at a two-week summer volleyball camp at the University of Montana when she was twelve years old. The first day was so exciting—getting registered, meeting

new people and feeling like the most independent 12-year-old in town—but then the camp began. The Grizzly collegiate players broke them into age groups and assured them that even beginners would be fine in their age bracket, which couldn't have been further from the truth for Katie.

The camp began with simple skill drills, just learning the basics, walking through the motions slowly and repeating them over and over—and Katie could not get one single thing right. She remembers thinking at the time that, "The majority of other 10-15-year-olds at this camp must've been playing in leagues for years," and for the very first time in her life, she was the one in the corner with a coach who was trying everything just to get her up to speed. At that point, Katie was terrified of even *trying* to learn the basics because she didn't want to be laughed at by the other girls.

Katie had played a number of other sports growing up and would humbly say that she had a natural athletic ability to pick up new athletic talents, but this camp proved to be the most degrading, enduring humiliating two weeks of her life to that point. She was "that" player, where every time the ball came to her, the drill would have to stop because of an error, and everyone's frustration (and laughter) seemed to be directed at her.

Katie's discomfort and humiliation didn't stop there: the friend that had invited her was playing much better than Katie and decided that she couldn't risk being seen as Katie's friend, so instead she avoided her at all costs, leaving her alone through a time of incredible frustration.

For the first week, Katie would find excuses to get out of drills and would call her mom constantly in tears begging to go home. Then a point came where the switch flipped and she found a way to channel this anxiety. She acknowledged that her fear of failure was actually greater than her feelings of frustration, abandonment, and humiliation, so by the second week she was flying all over the floor and putting in more effort than anyone else.

No, this story does not end with Katie being applauded for "most improved" or anything like that, but she did learn what it was like to feel so afraid to fail and then overcome it. In business, so often young people are thrown into situations that are uncomfortable or where they may lack confidence for the first time. By having gone through that experience at a young age in volleyball, Katie learned how to manage those feelings if they present themselves and how to best channel those emotions into positive energy.

Reminders about Learning to Make Mistakes

1. Remember, nobody is perfect. Everyone makes a mistake from time to time—the important thing is to learn from the mistake. If you make a mistake own it.

2. You often learn more from mistakes. Nothing like a back smack or a complete failure will motivate you to never to do it again.

3. If you become so risk adverse as to never make a mistake, then you aren't pushing yourself hard enough and may be stunting your professional growth.

4. Make your mistakes in practice; it's far less embarrassing then when it's for real. If you are embarrassed to make mistakes in front of others, it's best to do it in front of your teammates than an audience or client.

5. Face your fear head on; you'll be stronger because of it.

6. Look at failure as an opportunity to learn, grow and improve. It's not about getting knocked down, it's how you get back up.

7. Sometimes we fail unexpectedly and this can be quite emotional. Find a way to channel that failure into positive energy for improvement.

8. There will be times in your life when there will be people who are smarter, have more experience or are better at what you do than you are. This will be uncomfortable, but use your experiences overcoming the fear of failure to get past this.

Chapter 11: Grit

In both sports and business your courage to persevere and overcome (often referred to as grit) comes into play when times get hard. As an athlete, there can be times when you need to push through a small injury, play until the final whistle in a game you are losing, or push yourself in a conditioning drill when you are already exhausted. The resolve it takes to push through adversity in sports is much the same as that which is required in the business world. There are times when you have a deliverable due for a client and you need to put in the extra hours, or you know there is a mistake in your spreadsheet and you can't find it, so you need to keep looking and looking until you find the broken formula.

Grit is a descriptive characteristic because it demonstrates the strength of your character and that you are not willing to give up. While hard to measure, it is something learned in sports that can be of great help professionally, especially as more and more hiring managers are stating "grit" as one of the top characteristics that they are looking for in Millennial employees.

Grit Can Supplement Skill

Being a slower, weaker, 5' 7" athlete, Kevin wasn't the type of player that typically got recruited to play college soccer and in fact, when he showed up his first year, it was clear that out of the 64 players trying out for the soccer team, Kevin was the second worst player on the field.

However, what Kevin lacked in skill he made up with grit. Being short, he had to learn as a defender how to use his body to better position himself against taller attacking players. Not being the fastest person either, he had to learn to read a player's body language and anticipate their moves in order to break up a play or make a tackle. And not being particularly skilled (especially compared to the All-Americans on the team), Kevin had to put in many extra hours on his own to pick up the skills he needed to elevate his game. Where he couldn't attain the skills, he had to rely on his grit, aggressiveness and fitness to be able to compete against his opponents.

Grit is a trait he's had to rely on professionally multiple times. There have been times when he's been thrown onto a task where people have more experience and training, but his ability to dive head first into a task, research the heck out of it, and make sure that when he goes into a meeting that he is the most prepared person on the room pays off. This has become part of the SBC company culture and it is something that SBC looks for in its employees and even interns. SBC wants to hire employees that will give it their all, because being surrounded by people like that motivates everyone to do the same.

Discipline Doesn't Stop with Achievement
A former intern of SBC, Sierra Harden, has had to take and pass many tests in her martial arts career and now holds four black belts. She recalls these tests as being some of the hardest things she has ever done—which is saying something coming from a practicing martial artist of 15 years. Each belt test is designed to push you to the point of exhaustion which means you must be disciplined and have the mental fortitude to push through the pain. A common belief is once you achieve a black belt you have finished the journey and your belt becomes the symbol of your achievement. However, if you ask any martial artist, they will tell you that the discipline doesn't end there; you are just beginning to learn again.

This example demonstrates that even though she achieved what is commonly thought of as the highest achievement in martial arts, she doesn't plan on stopping there. Her foundation has been set, but it will take discipline to improve, teach, inspire and learn from others.

The same is true in a professional setting. Maybe you have received an amazing promotion, one that you have been vying for. Your hard work doesn't immediately cease because you have attained your goal—you were rewarded for your hard work and now the expectation is that you will produce even better results. The hard work you put in will be wasted if you end up slacking afterwards; therefore, maintaining your discipline to continue pushing forward is a skill that will benefit you throughout life.

Learning to Persevere Through Exhaustion
Katie's high school volleyball team held the state champion title her sophomore year and were runners up the following two—safe to say they were both revered and targeted by all other 4A high schools in the state. But the team didn't get the glory without having first learned what grit was all about, and how to persevere through mental and physical exhaustion.

Katie recalls two-a-days in the gym where they would have a personal trainer work them to the point of nausea at the start of their morning practices and then ask them to turn on a dime into meticulous skill drills requiring intense mental focus. After a break for lunch they would scrimmage through the afternoon where they had to attain a certain point total by performing specific plays in under 10 minutes, and every time they didn't reach the goal they would run suicides (sprints across the court) until they could finish the drill. You can imagine that it only got more and more difficult to pick her legs up between each set of suicides. Anyone who has played a sport knows the feeling of touching that last line and wanting to collapse, knowing that in 10 seconds the whistle was going to blow again and you better be ready to make that next play.

It did not feel worth it in the moment, but once game day rolled around and they were playing matches against rival schools, Katie and her team could run circles around their opponents. Their conditioning enabled them to hold their mental sharpness throughout the entire five-set match.

In the corporate world, you'll likely never have to run sprints or suicides, but there will come a time when you are sick, stressed or simply exhausted, and you will need to find a way to maintain your focus. During those moments, you may feel like your "to-do" list only gets longer and there will never be an end to the chaos and stress, but rest assured that the grit you developed from sports will serve you well.

Reminders about Grit

1. The courage to persevere and overcome is called grit. It is a skill that is built out of attitude.

2. Increasingly employers are looking for new hires that demonstrate grit and an attitude of perseverance to get the job done.

3. Once you achieve what you set out to do, the real test is what you do then. Continuing to work hard, teaching others and seeking to improve is what you need to do next.

4. If you are rewarded with a promotion or raise, that is a reflection as to what you've done, but there is an expectation that you will perform at an even higher level once you've realized this achievement.

5. By building up your endurance, when the crucial points arrive, you will be able to persevere through exhaustion in a way your opponents may not.

Conclusion

The purpose of this book was to help you, the reader, realize and recognize that you gained valuable life skills through your formative years either in the arts, by playing sports or both. We hope that the stories we shared from our lives are ones that you can relate to, because the characteristics and grit that were developed may not be hard skills that you can put on a resume, but they are intangible values that so many employers, co-workers and organizations are looking for.

And if you need to refer back to a story, we've compiled the key reminders from each section at the back of the book for reference.

Reminders from Each Chapter

These are reminders that we've pulled from each of the chapter's as a quick reference for you in certain situations. These are all pieces of advice we would give each other in the office as well as others who are seeking help for a specific situation.

Reminders for Exuding Confidence

1. Hold your head high, smile and make eye contact with each corner of the room.

2. Positive self-talk: This is a great way to help yourself feel more confident about the presentation or performance. Try telling yourself, "I'm going to rock this presentation!"

3. Visualize where you are most relaxed, happy and calm and then find a way to overlay that onto whatever situation you are in. This will help you squash your feelings of doubt.

4. Don't let on to your audience if you are nervous. Fake it until you make it!

5. Dress for success: Time after time, studies show that those who look the part feel more confident in themselves and will give off a sense of confidence and expertise to others around them.

Reminders for Preparation and Discipline

1. Sometimes you "just don't feel like practicing." Create a schedule of times to prepare during the week and stick to it. Schedule yourself enough time to prepare adequately.

2. Expect the unexpected. Create a list of all the things that could go wrong and prepare for them. This anticipation will enable you to handle them more professionally if/when they do come up.

3. If you're nervous or concerned, practice and put in the effort to get it right! There are no shortcuts.

4. If you're working on a team, being independently disciplined is crucial to your team's success. If you have a conflict that disables you from preparing adequately, communicate that to your team so they can cover.

Reminders for Working in Teams

1. Communicate ahead of time. In groups, talk and prepare for who is doing what, when and learn non-verbal cues.

2. Tailor your role within the team and how it fits into the overall final deliverable. There will be times when you are the leader and driver, and times when your role is more supportive.

3. Sometimes you'll need to speak louder or bring energy to a room to gain attention from the audience—but never do this to outshine your teammates.

4. Recognize those times when you may need to soften your voice to be more in-line with your group so that the teams message isn't lost to the audience by one person.

5. Make decisions as a team to allow for innovation, new ideas and to avoid conflict and animosity towards teammates.

Reminders to Remain Calm and Improvise

1. Breathe and remain calm, avoid any type of indication that you have just made a mistake. The audience may not notice unless you clue them in.

2. Ad-lib or improvise when needed. Oftentimes this is the best savior for a mistake during a performance.

3. If it's appropriate, make a small joke regarding your mistake. In a business setting, this can lighten the mood in the room.

4. If something crucial is missed during a presentation DO NOT call out yours or a fellow colleague's mishap. Simply reiterate and apologize for leaving the information out.

5. Most importantly, realize that everyone makes mistakes more often than not—it's how you manage the mistake that either turns the audience for or against you.

Reminders for Reconciling Clashing Styles

1. Have open communication about work styles, norms and goals.

2. Be aware and understanding of someone else's style and figure out how best to complement one another and maximize each other's strengths.

3. To avoid conflict, try switching up habits from time to time so everyone feels as if their work norm is being appreciated.

4. Be true to yourself, but realize sometimes we might all need to adjust our styles for the greater good.

5. Realize that some time you may be set up for failure from the beginning in terms of style. Make sure you find an environment that will enable you to succeed.

Reminders for How to Work with a Difficult Person

1. If it's a difficult colleague or peer, try and get to the root cause of the problem and understand the "why" behind the conflict.

2. If they are an instructor/manager, be sure to be true to yourself and explain what isn't working.

3. Realize that if a co-worker is unreliable and untrustworthy, sometimes you just have to move on and find a way to work around them.

Reminders about Leadership

1. Sports put you in a fast paced, ever changing, competitive environment, so the leadership experience you gain in sports is applicable in business or a start-up environment as well.

2. It's important to be true to who you are and lead in the manner that you are most comfortable.

3. Leadership takes many different forms, some lead by example, others motivate verbally, while others sit back and observe. All are valid methods and various forms may be needed at different times. People need different types of leadership and it's important to know when to provide which kind.

4. Organizational leadership requires delegation.

5. Not everyone responds to the same leadership style. Effective leaders tailor their message and style to the people they are trying to lead to what works best for those individuals.

6. Leadership involves empathy and can sometimes mean caring more about the individual you are leading than the immediate goal in the short-term.

Reminders about the Importance of Strategy, Anticipation and Preparation

1. Expect the unexpected.

2. It's all in the preparation. If you have a strategy with a backup plan, you can better adjust on the fly or when adversity strikes. Failing to prepare can lead to stress and a lesser performance, there is no excuse for not being prepared.

3. Know your audience. Try and anticipate their questions, concerns and issues before you step into a meeting or give a presentation.

4. You don't know where you are going until you know where you are. Assess your position first before creating a strategy forward.

5. To beat a tougher opponent, there is no short cut to putting in the hard work and extra time.

6. You will face headwinds; sometimes all it takes is a simple jive or a tack to get the wind to start working for you as opposed to against you.

7. Sometimes preparation and anticipation can overcome skill and experience. Prepare vigorously for your time to come, so when the opportunity does present itself, you are ready to seize it.

8. If you are young and you are meeting with someone older or more experienced, one way to level the playing field is to over prepare and know everything about the organization, individuals and industry before walking through the door.

Reminders about Knowing Your Role

1. The best teams function when everyone's role is clear. Establish roles early on so that there is no confusion.

2. Clear communication on roles can help alleviate anxiety, jealousy and concern from teammates ahead of time.

3. One's role can change in an instant, which can lead to confusion. To get over this, one must understand what is required in a new role and why. Being able to be flexible in the short term or in a pinch is important.

4. When a role changes, your mindset about the person you are doesn't have to change, but it may just manifest itself differently. This doesn't mean you skills or talents have been lost, but rather, they are just being utilized differently.

5. Sometimes you must embrace a leadership role, even if you don't want to or don't have the confidence to do so. If that is what is required by your team, sometimes you have to step up for the greater good.

6. Sometimes the most important people on a team are the ones behind the scenes who rarely get the glory.

Reminders about Learning to Make Mistakes

1. Remember, nobody is perfect. Everyone makes a mistake from time to time—the important thing is to learn from the mistake. If you make a mistake own it.

2. You often learn more from mistakes. Nothing like a back smack or a complete failure will motivate you to never to do it again.

3. If you become so risk adverse as to never make a mistake, then you aren't pushing yourself hard enough and may be stunting your professional growth.

4. Make your mistakes in practice; it's far less embarrassing then when it's for real. If you are embarrassed to make mistakes in front of others, it's best to do it in front of your teammates than an audience or client.

5. Face your fear head on; you'll be stronger because of it.

6. Look as failure as an opportunity to learn, grow and improve. It's not about getting knocked down, it's how you get back up.

7. Sometimes we fail unexpectedly and this can be quite emotional. Find a way to channel that failure into positive energy for improvement.

8. There will be times in your life when there will be people who are smarter, have more experience or are better at what you do than you are. This will be uncomfortable, but use your experiences overcoming the fear of failure to get past this.

Reminders about Grit

1. The courage to persevere and overcome is
    called grit. It is a skill that is built out of
    attitude.

2. Increasingly, employers are looking for
    new hires that demonstrate grit and an
    attitude of perseverance to get the job
    done.

3. Once you achieve what you set out to do,
    the real test is what you do then.
    Continuing to work hard, teaching others
    and seeking to improve is what you need to
    do next.

4. If you are rewarded with a promotion or
    raise, that is a reflection as to what you've
    done, but there is an expectation that you
    will perform at an even higher level once
    you've realized this achievement.

5. By building up your endurance, when the crucial points arrive, you will be able to persevere through exhaustion in a way your opponents may not.

Acknowledgements

We all want to thank a few people.

Kevin: I want to thank my parents for the ability to write this book. Mostly because they were the ones who supported me during my childhood, through high school and college as I learned, struggled, enjoyed and balanced all my artistic and sport activities with my academics and a very fun social life.

Mom and Dad, you provided me with the opportunities, the financial and emotional support and the encouragement when I needed it most. Above it all, thank you for always being at so many of my games and performances. You truly gave me the wings to fly and I love you.

I also want to thank my wife JO who has been my absolute best friend, love of my life, and rock by my side. Thank you for always believing in me and encouraging me to do more. I also want to thank George and Valerie Opdyke, as well as all my coaches, teammates, choir members and cast mates who make things fun and lively; I have some great memories because of you.

Annie: I want to start off by saying thank you to my parents who have always pushed me in anything that I did—whether it was sports, my singing career or school, I have always felt supported. You've enabled me to be successful and given me the tools and resources to hone my skills and interests. I wouldn't be where I am in life without your guidance and teachings of dedication. Thank you for coming to all my games, even when I was injured and couldn't step on the field, and to all my performances even when you were busy.

I also want to thank my sister, Emily Thomas, for being a motivator to me. Although you may not know it, you pushed me to be better as well and to be more comfortable on stage—you're my duet partner for life. Lastly, I want to thank my Aunt Darlene and Uncle Ken who have served as second parents to me and lent support in both my sports and singing career. Aunt Darlene, I will never forget the day you ran to the rest of the family in excitement asking them if they knew I could sing. For the rest that have supported my endeavors—seen me play soccer or sing—thank you so much, I love you all!

Ruth: I would like to thank my parents for their full-hearted support in all my interests, whether it be paying for lessons, driving me from practice to practice (patiently waiting in the car the whole time!), taking up tennis just to practice with me and always pushing me to be my best.

I also want to thank all the tennis partners I've had along the years for the invaluable gifts of partnership: working together tightly as a team of two and for the many laughs and friendships for a lifetime. And to my piano teachers, thank you for your patience and undivided enthusiasm for when I felt discouraged. Without your guidance and continuous message that "practice makes perfect" I would not be where I am today. Thank you!

Katie: To my most incredible parents, thank you. Thank you for the early mornings, the long tournament days, the loads of laundry and somehow always having that extra granola bar on hand. Thank you for buying a van to take me and my teammates to and from practice. Thank you for giving me unparalleled guidance and support. I've learned more about good character and what it means to love unconditionally by simply watching you two.

I'd like to thank my fiancé, Michael Secrist, for being my better half and reminding me to take the time for self-reflection, for encouraging me to reach my best self and beyond. I also want to thank my coaches and my teammates from Rain City Volleyball Club and especially from Jackson High School. Between the floor burns and two-a-days, the sing-a-long bus rides and late nights in hotel rooms, I have so much to thank you for: friendships, mentorships, memories, role models and more.

[i] Chapman University 2015 Study on American Fears
https://blogs.chapman.edu/wilkinson/2015/10/13/americas
-top-fears-2015/
[ii] Deloitte Millennial Survey 2016:
https://www2.deloitte.com/content/dam/Deloitte/global/D
ocuments/About-Deloitte/gx-millenial-survey-2016-exec-
summary.pdf
[iii] Journal of Leadership and Organizational Studies:
Sports At Work
http://journals.sagepub.com/doi/abs/10.1177/15480518145
38099